SCRE

presents

VIDEO GAME VAULT

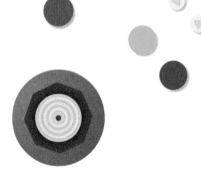

the *best** of

NINTENDO 64 ™

Copyright © 2016 by ScrewAttack (Craig Skistimas, Bryan Baker, Nick Cramer, Chad James, Shaun Bolen, Sam Mitchell, Ben Singer, Sean Hinz, and Austin Harper)

Published by Mango Media Inc.

Front and Back Cover, Interior Design, Illustrations, Theme and Layout: Roberto Núñez.

Additional Images by Henry Perez

Copy Editor: Jessica Davis

Content Editor: Hugo Villabona

ISBN 978-1-63353-373-8

"For young players, classic games are brand new. For older players, they bring back memories and make you feel good."

– Satoru Iwata

Dedication

This book is dedicated to our families and
friends who we played games with and who
encouraged us to follow our dreams, the amazing
ScrewAttack g1 community, and everyone who's
ever picked up an N64 and smiled.

CONTENTS

Introduction   **8**

Austin   **12**

Perfect Dark (2000)   14

Pokémon Snap (1999)   18

Ben   22

The Legend Of Zelda: Ocarina Of Time (1998)   24

Super Smash Bros. (1999)   26

Mario Party 2 (2000)   29

Pokémon Stadium (2000)   31

Star Fox 64 (1997)   33

Bryan   36

Battletanx (1998)   38

Bomberman 64 (1997)   41

Fighting Force 64 (1997)   45

Wcw/Nwo Revenge (1998)   49

Chad   **54**

1080° Snowboarding (1998)   56

Buck Bumble (1998)   60

Conker's Bad Fur Day (2001)   63

Diddy Kong Racing (1997)   66

Goldeneye 007 (1997)   70

Mario Party (1998)   73

Rush 2: Extreme Racing Usa (1998)   76

Craig   **80**

Cruis'n Usa (1996)   82

Mario Kart 64 (1997)   85

Nba Hangtime (1997)   88

Nfl Blitz 2000 (1999)   91

Yoshi's Story (1998)   94

Nick   98
Banjo-Kazooie (1998)   100
The Legend Of Zelda: Majora's Mask (2000)   103
Kirby 64: The Crystal Shards (2000)   106
Blast Corps (1997)   108
Sam   110
Donkey Kong 64 (1999)   112
F-Zero X (1998)   116
Harvest Moon 64 (1999)   119
Jet Force Gemini (1999)   122
Pilotwings 64 (1996)   125
Snowboard Kids (1998)   128
Star Wars: Rogue Squadron (1998)   131
Sean   136
Gauntlet Legends (1999)   138
Hydro Thunder (2000)   141
Turok: Dinosaur Hunter (1997)   144
Wave Race 64 (1996)   147
Winback: Covert Operations (1999)   150
Ogre Battle 64: Person Of Lordly Caliber (2000)   153
Shaun   156
Star Wars Episode I: Racer (1999)   158
Mario Tennis (2000)   161
Super Mario 64 (1996)   163
Star Wars: Shadows Of The Empire (1996)   166
Beetle Adventure Racing (1999)   168
Extreme-G (1997)   170
The Vault   172
Author Bio   174

INTRODUCTION

As I thought about ways to start this book, all I wanted to say over and over again was "the N64 is awesome," and I couldn't quite find a good way of saying it. So after thinking long and hard about it while watching some professional wrestling, I thought, "why not just say it?" So allow me to put this as eloquently as possible: **THE N64 IS AWESOME.**

If you were to add up all the time we've spent with consoles at ScrewAttack over the years I would guess that we've easily spent more time with the N64 than any other system. There are just SO MANY good games to play on it, and that's exactly why we wanted to celebrate it with this book. Make no mistake, this book is not a list of the *best* games ever on the N64. Actually, some of the games in this book aren't good at all; however, that doesn't mean we don't love them. These are simply the games we're most connected to on Nintendo's third console.

The fact is, here at ScrewAttack, we're just a bunch of folks who love video games for a variety of reasons. So we thought we'd write this book as a group, with each person taking a few entries to talk about their choices.

HOW TO HOLD AN N64 CONTROLLER

Most of us were smart in the 1990s; some of us were not. Like the Neanderthals before us that consulted dinosaurs on tricky topics, we consulted manuals. At no point in history was this consultation process more important. Those of us that did read our literature knew how to hold the N64's odd controller – with a kind of poise only previously seen at aristocratic tea parties. Those who chose not to become enlightened could be spotted a mile away by the pure inefficiency of their controller hold —plebeians at heart— and this mark of shame never left.

The Right Way

This is the correct way to hold an N64 controller. There is no argument against this.

The Wrong Way (Most of the Time)

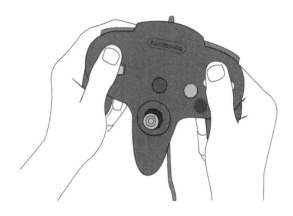

While some people may argue this hold style is efficient, or even suggested by the manual for some games, they are wrong. Any person or game developer unwilling to adapt to the clearly more efficient joystick system while clinging onto their precious directional pad has certainly been left behind in the 20th century.

Disclaimer – It can be argued that some gameplay would benefit from holding the controller in an unorthodox manner. Be warned, however, that partaking in awkward-controlling may result in lifelong ridicule. Play at your own risk.

The WTF-Are-You-Doing Way

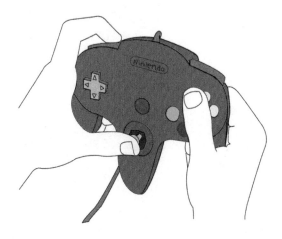

There is simply no argument for this grandiose misuse. Often when a person was found holding a controller like this they were burned at the stake, an overly gracious punishment for such a heinous crime.

AUSTIN

Austin has led multiple video game launches for the ScrewAttack Games brand and more recently had the pleasure of bringing one of ScrewAttack's own games to Nintendo home consoles. He looks back fondly on the N64 era as a time that shaped his childhood and fostered his competitive spirit, despite being a filthy Sony fanboy.

@PotatoHound

PERFECT DARK
(2000)

When I was a child, I was forced to make the very difficult decision between owning a PlayStation or an Nintendo 64. Because I was raised as a Sega kid and brainwashed with the mantra "Nintendon't," I went with the PlayStation and have never looked back. Fortunately for me, my younger brother received a Nintendo 64 during Christmas of '99, so I did eventually get to enjoy most of the classics.

Now, for those of you who grew up without a sibling rivalry, I can never fully describe the joy that comes from dominating your brother in his own game, on his own console... but it's pretty much the best. Crushing his offensive line in *NFL Blitz 2000* or giving him the ol' Stone Cold Stunner in *WWF No Mercy* was always pretty satisfying, but nothing will ever compare to mowing him down with a Laptop Gun in *Perfect Dark*.

Assuming you missed out on this classic, *Perfect Dark* was Rare's follow up to the 1997 hit *GoldenEye*, and it improved upon its predecessor in nearly every way – especially in its intelligent NPC AI, which is like 90 percent of the challenge in most single-player FPS's anyway. The single-player campaign allowed players to take on the role of the badass secret agent, Joanna Dark, in her attempt to save the world from an evil corporation and a bloodthirsty alien race. The real reason people played the game was for the multiplayer.

The game came loaded with a multitude of preset multiplayer modes that could be unlocked by playing increasingly difficult challenges. On top of that, the combat simulator also allowed players to set custom parameters for almost all aspects of the match.

Between setting the AI behaviors, customizing weapon loadouts, changing objectives, game modes, match lengths, and choosing your favorite maps and soundtracks it was virtually impossible to get bored of destroying your opponents.

It was a fantastic and enjoyable game (no doubt) but to fully understand why I hold *Perfect Dark* so dear you must know that my brother and I also used its multiplayer combat simulator as a sort of "trial by video game" system for gambling off chores and settling debates. *Perfect Dark* was the law around my house as a kid and I honestly cannot begin to fathom the amount of time I spent practicing this game just so I could bask in having defeated him. Sure, mastering the strange controller layout may have crippled me from ever being able to right-stick well in any future FPS, but I live with no regrets. *Perfect Dark* was one of the greatest multiplayer shooters of its time and is hands down one of the best games ever made for the Nintendo 64.

POKÉMON
SNAP (1999)

You remember those really crappy "games" that you used to find hiding deep in your Cap'n Crunch or partnered with your delicious pepperoni pizza? You know, those horrible franchise tie-ins that companies used to push on us, assuming we didn't know what they were really up to? That's what came to mind the first time I held *Pokémon Snap* in my hands. Looking down at the box, I could only assume that Kodak had licensed Pokémon and paid off some poor developer to push more disposable cameras. Then again, it had all my favorite Pokémon rendered in glorious 3-D. Needless to say, I had mixed emotions. Imagine my surprise then, when this rail shooter became one of the most beloved games of my childhood.

For those of you who've never had the fortune of playing the game, let me explain. *Pokémon Snap* is a magical and wonderful game of safari-style photography set in the Pokémon universe. The mechanics of the game seem simple enough: you shoot Pokémon with a camera, not a gun (though that just might have made an even better game). As you traverse the land in the trusty Zero-One buggy (armed with only a camera, some apples, a flute, and a sack full of Pester Balls), it is your mission to take the very best photographs of Pokémon in their natural habitats for Professor Oak's research. Oak, the lazy, old bastard who can never do anything for himself, judges you harshly on your photography skills, awarding extra points for stupid things like "frame composition" and "being able to see the entire Pokémon."

For me, the pinnacle of enjoyment in *Pokémon Snap* came from being hypercompetitive. By using the items provided and mastering your snap skills, you could spend all day replacing your friend's lower-scoring photographs with epic masterpieces like "Pikachu on a Surfboard," or my personal favorite, "Ceci est une Fleur de la Joie." After delivering your superior works of art to Professor Oak, you could drive to the local Blockbuster, print out your Pulitzer-winning masterpiece from your save cartridge, and stick it to your friend's refrigerator for his whole family to admire for years to come.

Aside from being a great game, *Pokémon Snap* helped spark my passion for photography and filmography, eventually inspiring me to pursue it as a major in college. Sure, I immediately changed majors after learning that my professor didn't believe in Oak's grading system (and that most models don't enjoy being pelted with apples), but *Pokémon Snap* forever holds a place in my heart. It is one of the few N64 games that I will still go out of my way to play today. Honestly, a sequel with realistic textures would be a much welcomed addition to my hypothetical VR library.

Tell me you wouldn't shit yourself if a giant Gyarados came at you from behind a waterfall in a beautiful, fully immersive 3-D world. Yeah, let's get on that.

BEN

Ben has been in the video game and entertainment industry since high school. The N64 was his first gaming console. His love of *Super Smash Bros.* may have inspired his hit web show, *Death Battle*, because who doesn't love seeing all sorts of crazy characters in ridiculous brawls?

@ScrewAttackBen

THE LEGEND OF ZELDA: OCARINA OF TIME (1998)

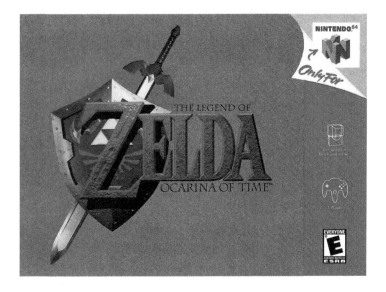

The best game ever made. At least that's what the Internet would have you believe. The Internet would also have you believe that you should never trust the Internet. Whether I was traversing the tallest mountains or exploring the darkest dungeon, the best thing about *Zelda* games to me was the sense of adventure I got while playing. Unfortunately, the worlds of 8- and 16-bit *Zelda* just didn't pull me in enough. The kingdom of Hyrule can only be so interesting when it's just a bunch of trees, caves, and dirt copied and pasted over and over. Then *Ocarina*

of Time happened and BAM! The world of Hyrule came alive! Even though this was the first 3-D *Zelda* game, the characters, swordplay, and puzzle-solving translated perfectly.

Plus, for the first time the epic adventure truly did feel epic, like something you would actually see on a movie screen. But I'll never forget exploring the world for the first time and suddenly realizing just how big this game was! It was an adventure and a half just walking across Hyrule Field! When the sun came down, skeleton monsters would crawl from the ground. Looking back, they were rather harmless enemies, but at the time my 9-year-old self dreaded every moment the sun wasn't up! Thank god for speedy horseback riding.

SUPER SMASH BROS. (1999)

Super Smash Bros. is the most important game from my childhood. Before the bowling power of the Wii changed their minds, my parents were rather hesitant about having video games in the house when I was a kid. Gaming consoles were still a relatively new thing and they feared that constant gaming and staring at a TV screen would be unhealthy for a young child.

Hell, the fact they bought my brother and I *Pokémon* and Game Boys seemed like an honest-to-god miracle. However, my family never owned an NES, Genesis, or SNES, so I got most of my gaming fix by going over to my friends' houses and sitting in front of their TVs for hours— much to the annoyance of their parents. Then one day my hair got really shaggy and my mom took me to a hair salon called Cool Cuts. I know that sounds completely out of left field but it's important, dammit! The gimmick with Cool Cuts was that while you got your haircut, you could play a video game... and they had a Nintendo 64 with *Smash Bros.*! This was my first taste of playing not just *Smash*, but the N64 itself.

I distinctly remember choosing Pikachu and spamming Thunder Shock over and over until I got stuck on Fox's stage. Naturally, hearing Pikachu scream his name over and over and getting my ass kicked by a fox with a laser gun on a spaceship inspired me to begin a campaign for my own Nintendo 64. It only takes... I dunno... 10 minutes max to trim a 9-year-old boy's hair? That wasn't nearly enough time! I needed more of that *Smash 64* goodness! I wanted to try blasting Mario across Hyrule Castle with Samus' arm cannon, pile drive Captain Falcon off the edge of Yoshi's Island with Kirby, defeat the giant Mickey Mouse hand that showed up at the end of the game for some reason... Lo and behold, on Christmas Day of 1999, my parents gave in and finally allowed a Nintendo console in the house. Thank you, *Smash Bros*. Oh, and the game's pretty good too. Though I wouldn't become obsessed with *Smash* until the next generation.

MARIO PARTY 2 (2000)

Mario Party 1 was really fun, right? Whoever at Nintendo came up with the bizarre idea of turning Mario into a board game with challenges straight out of a reality TV show was probably a strange kind of genius, but a genius nonetheless. He was also a masochist for making us have to spin the N64's analog stick round and round and round so fast our thumbs bled. *Mario Party 2* fixed all that!

It delivered everything that made the original *Mario Party* great and made it better. I'm probably in the minority when I say that, but I honestly think this is the best of the Mario parties. I even really liked the themed getups, like Western Land and Pirate Land. Plus, this took the minigame Bumper Balls from *Mario*

Party 1, aka the best minigame made in the history of ever, and somehow made it even better! How does that even happen?

POKÉMON STADIUM (2000)

Nowadays, the temptation of a fully 3-D Pokémon adventure has been a recurring request from thousands of Pokémon fans around the globe. But when all we had to play was *Pokémon Red, Blue,* and *Yellow,* a 3-D Pokémon wasn't really in high demand.

Then Nintendo blew everyone's minds with *Pokémon Stadium*! All those unique and colorful creatures we'd been battling and training on our tiny Game Boys were now in full color, full 3-D on our TVs! And best of all, *Pokémon Stadium* came with a Transfer Pack add-on, a device that plugged into the N64 controller and could house your *Pokémon* game cartridge, letting you bring the very Pokémon team you spent weeks and weeks training on your Game Boy and witness them on the TV!

The Transfer Pack also let you play your Pokémon Game Boy game on the TV like the Super Game Boy did on the SNES but it only worked for Pokémon games, which really disappointed me. Then there was a minigame where you flipped a helpless Magikarp into the air over and over to hit a button. So... let's just say *Pokémon Stadium* had its fair share of highs and lows.

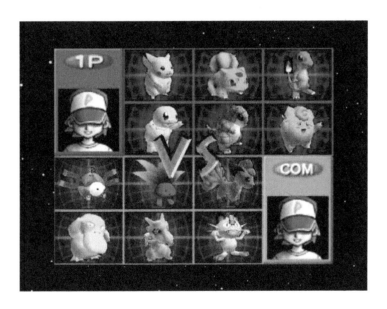

STAR FOX 64
(1997)

Growing up, I was really into *Star Wars*. Like... scarily so. I had the toys, collected the comics, read the novels, and of course, played the video games. But not even *Rogue Squadron* delivered the true dogfighting-in space action I really wanted. Little did I know I'd find it in a game where a fox and his animal friends fight a giant decapitated monkey in space.

Tight controls, awesome boss fights, charming characters, memorable music, quotable one-liners, multiple variations to missions, quirky teammates... This game had everything I wanted. Plus it had voice acting! To my knowledge, this is one of the first (if not the first) console game to have every line of dialogue completely voiced. This alone made the characters in

Star Fox 64 unique in the best way possible; everything felt like it could fit nicely into a Saturday morning cartoon. Which for some reason doesn't exist even though it would be basically the best thing ever. That's a fact, obviously.

Nostalgia and charm blinders be damned, *Star Fox 64* is perfect. Not really in a "this game has no flaws" way, but in a "no matter how many times I play this game I will always have fun" way. I like *Star Fox 64* way too much.

BRYAN

A longtime writer for the *Video Game Vault* series on ScrewAttack.com. There wasn't a day in 7th grade that Bryan didn't spend playing multiplayer games on the Nintendo 64. That *Wrestlemania 2000* cartridge got a llllooootttt of use. A. Lot.

@tehrealbryan

BATTLETANX

(1998)

BattleTanx holds a special place in my heart for a variety of reasons, and the first is definitely the uber-cheesy plot. IN THE DISTANT FUTURE OF 2001, some crazy disease is killing off all the women in America, eventually leaving a gender ratio of one thousand men to a single woman.

The majority of women have been taken to quarantined safety in San Francisco, leaving lots of lonely men and a dwindling supply of lotion to fend for themselves. Among these men is one Griffin Spade, who with the help of his beloved Madison would've created a baby with the strongest cheekbones in all of recorded history. However, Madison was also taken from New York City. In time, a vaccination is found to cure the lady-killer virus, and women begin to make their way back out into what remains of the U.S.

Since the outbreak, the entire government collapsed and now tribes of what are basically motorized cavemen roam the land. What women there are in the wasteland are prized possessions for these tribes called "Queenlords," and Griffin wants to get his back.

In *BattleTanx* it's like Oprah's dying wish was to give everyone a tank. It's the only way I could ever figure that every lunatic and biker gang in the contiguous forty-eight states got ahold of a bunch of war machines.

QUEENS, NEW YORK · MARCH 23, 2001

I'll thank whoever decided to hyper-escalate the right to bear arms because blowing up America is a blast (pun totally intended). These tanks can really move on the Nintendo 64. And whether it's the campaign or multiplayer, the action can get pretty intense.

Straight up Deathmatch, Last Man Standing, and Capture the Flag/Queenlord were some great times back in the day. The Goliath Tanks that guard the different groups' bases are super tough, even if for some reason they're stuck on a track and move like they took their defense strategy from *Space Invaders*. Regardless, Griffin's army is basically glorified cannon fodder against those things. We all want to go get our ladies back but you gotta stay alive, guys!

To top it off, *BattleTanx* has one of the best video game commercials of all time. That silly little bear really got the stuffing knocked out of it! What did it think it was doing trying to sell laundry detergent in the world of *BattleTanx*? We got a classic *Clip of the Week* out of it, Craig got a nickname, and we got a phrase that lives to this very day: "We don't. Take. BREAKS!!!!" *BattleTanx* is a classic all the way around.

BOMBERMAN 64 (1997)

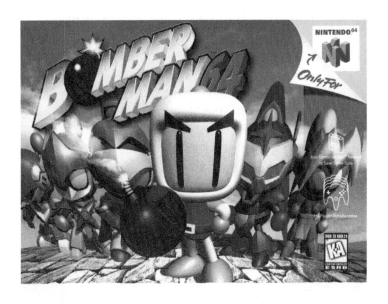

Let's talk about a game that is a blast to play: *Bomberman 64*. Some people at ScrewAttack will heap praise on its Adventure Mode, but it's not why you played this game. Spending too much time in Adventure Mode is like going to the salad bar at a Brazilian steakhouse more than once. It gets you ready for the main course, gets you a custom outfit that doesn't affect gameplay, and it takes time away from the bacon-wrapped filet mignon. That's not why I plugged that cartridge in. I came for the endless onslaught of meaty goodness that is the Battle Mode.

I never entered that steakhouse/*Bomberman 64* level alone, either. No, I brought a few friends, because this is something meant to be enjoyed in good company.

Every round of Battle Mode action was only made sweeter by the audible frustration of the person you just ghosted. I always kept my head on a swivel afterwards though, since the person I just killed was definitely not out. They could repay my explosive generosity by haunting my butt right into someone else's bomb. It was the piggyback ride I never wanted to give. It doesn't always look like it, but after playing *Bomberman 64* for a while, there were these little strategies that began to appear.

Trying to predict someone's movements or corral them with bombs gave wins that extra bit of satisfaction. Catching that jerk kid from down the street with the best-kicked bomb I'd swung my digital foot into all summer felt a little more special. If you could grab the brat who broke your favorite Transformer and throw him over the ledge, no bomb needed? Even better.

Sometimes that little punk got lucky though and managed to snag a piece of Evil or transfer his Plague modifier to me.

Giving everyone powered-up red bombs was one thing. Making me really big and really slow meant they weren't invited to the next sleepover. With the power of the third dimension, the fates of elementary friendships were no longer flat affairs. The rock garden was a good introductory level, the one we all knew but in 3-D. Things got interesting after that, because the newfound depth could be a total death trap if you were out of your depth. Blizzard Battle and Field of Grass particularly stand out for their own diabolical reasons. No one bothered to mow Field so when people weren't looking out, my bombs could totally sneak up on them.

Blizzard Battle was a total wildcard because my bombs might go any way the wind blows. Doesn't really matter to me though, because my pumped-up power bombs take out half the map anyway. I blew everyone up.

FIGHTING FORCE 64 (1997)

This entry in the *Video Game Vault* is coming from a place of 2-D side scrolling beat' em up love. *TMNT*, *The Simpsons*, *Final Fight*, *Street of Rage*, *Aliens vs Predator*, and a bunch more could fill a kid's afternoon with all the sprite-based pugilism they could ask for. But as it happened with many popular franchises and genres, the jump into the third dimension was not always a graceful one. Sacrifices were made for the pixels, and games like *Fighting Force 64* just weren't quite what we hoped for.

Fighting Force 64 is a pretty straightforward port of a game that had already been out for two years on the PlayStation. Its original publisher, Eidos Interactive, was so "meh" on the idea of going through the publishing process for *Fighting Force* a second time that they dropped the game. If it weren't for Crave stepping in, N64 owners may have never been exposed to a game that they played then just sort of dropped before moving on with their lives. Everything about the game is so by the numbers, beginning with its self-explanatory title. Some crazy old guy thinks he's going to kick off the apocalypse so it's up to me to fight and force my way into stopping him. Who's up for the task?

A scantily clad gumshoe, a bad guy with a heart of gold, the prisoner he bribes the nearby prison to loan out for missions, and a raver who is tripping balls on justice, that's who! Only the crazy guy's army of minions (who all pretty much fight the same way) stand in your way; that's a problem on top of another problem. There just wasn't much variety in the action. Every level and fight went about the same way, no one was juggling knives on fire or anything. *Die Hard Arcade*, a game you could play over on the Saturn, at least had juggling knives. *Fighting Force 64* was slow and boring. Beat' em ups were born in the arcades, where quick pacing and action sucked all the quarters out of your pockets. It was like someone wanted to make a dark and gritty beat' em up, and in the process ignore everything that made the genre fun.

Comparing it to those 2-D games mentioned at the top, *Fighting Force* just didn't compare. Kids got *Fighting Force* for Christmas or their birthday or whatever, played for a bit, then went back to their *Streets of Rage*. People didn't have their heads so far up their butts at the time that the idea of a game running at 60 frames per second was a justifiable excuse for a game that was immaculately average. After the PlayStation release, Core had two years to read reviews and fan feedback and fix things, such as "tightening up the graphics."

But they didn't, so all N64 owners got was a cartridge full of "meh."

WCW/NWO REVENGE (1998)

Being a fan of professional wrestling in general was great back in the 90s. The Monday Night Wars were raging, and one place WCW had a clear advantage was in video games with *WCW/nWo Revenge*. Think about it, try to name a 3-D wrestling game Acclaim made for the WWF that could hold a candle to this game changer. It. Is. NOT. Possible. THQ and Aki didn't just raise the bar, they put it in the stratosphere.

They gave us a game that even the "you know wrestling is fake, right?" crowd can't deny enjoying. Being a very approachable game went a long way in keeping players engaged. B attacks and A does grapples, then how long the button is held can change whether the move is normal or stronger. That's pretty easy to understand.

You could describe the rest to your buddy as necessary the longer your first matches lasted.

The game just unfolded in front of new players and kept pulling them deeper with each command that seemed simple, yet was actually interactive and engaging. It helped that WCW at the time had a pretty diverse roster, so with the fighting games ruling the arcades, everyone could find someone to play with. Guys like Hulk Hogan, Randy Savage, Bret Hart, Lex Luger, and British Bulldog had made the move from WWF so those were familiar names. WCW had made its own big names like Sting, naked Goldberg (if you give him the gold trunks), and Booker T. Or Perhaps the oddballs like Disco Inferno or Raven did it for you.

Maybe the luchadores like Rey Mysterio, La Parka, or Psychosis were more your style. If all else failed, call me crazy, you could go with the guy largely responsible for this game's title, Scott Hall. The boxy style created on the N64 only accentuated the biceps of Lex Luger and Big Poppa Pump himself, Scott Steiner. Sting and Randy Savage actually had authentic voice clips to go with their taunts. Someone at THQ thought that was worth including, and they were right. You could bust everyone wide open and bloody, everyone had their signature moves, the replay system highlighted them well, and getting three of your buddies to experience this with you was a blast.

Every time that one friend couldn't figure out why he kept taking wakeup shots to the crotch was a moment to revel in. It was always the end of an era when they realized that puffing their chest out to "block" somehow turned their wrestling trunks into an iron curtain. But even after that, every so often, that bell would still go.

Getting to step between the ropes at Starcade, Halloween Havoc, Bash at the Beach, Great American Bash, and Monday Night Nitro (to name a few) was a blast and still is! We still bust out our Revenge cart on a pretty regular basis at the ScrewAttack HQ, more so than its successors. That old Acclaim stuff back at the beginning? No one thinks twice about it. *WWF War Zone*? More like show them the door zone.

Revenge was so good WWF locked down THQ and Aki after this classic game and got some great titles themselves, but we can't ignore where it all started. *WCW/nWo Revenge* is just too sweet.

CHAD

Chad James is the Senior Manager of Brand for ScrewAttack.com and has been a lifelong video game fan. He's been playing games since 1989, and his favorite console of all time is the Nintendo 64! He believes games are better when you can share them with your friends and the N64 was a console that championed that.

@ScrewAttackChad

1080°
SNOWBOARDING
(1998)

I remember popping in *1080° Snowboarding* for the first time. I flipped on my N64's power switch and as my awaiting face was basked in the glory of the red light of the power button, I was greeted with three meaty power chords from an electric guitar, followed by that stereotypical 90s announcer voice saying "Ten Eighty!" A big grin crossed my face and I couldn't wait to get started. The game wasted no time in tossing me straight into the action. All I had to do was choose my mode, snowboarder, and board and start shredding. If I wanted to race, I could take on the computer or go head-to-head against one of my friends. Or I could challenge myself in Time Attack, trying to perfect my race time.

I spent hours finding all the hidden pathways in each course that allowed me to cut down my time and speed past my friends. But for me, this game was all about tricks. Just as a skateboarder's tricks are paramount, I was always playing Trick Attack or practicing in Training Mode, trying to cruise the halfpipe and put together a solid trick run. The reason? The trick system in the game was actually quite difficult, and that difficulty is one of the things that makes the game great! It required you to memorize a series of button combinations to pull off the best stuff. Grabs were relatively easy, all I had to do was hold B and a direction, but to pull off the coveted 1080 of the game's namesake I couldn't just hold the stick in one direction. Oh no, I had to input R+360 analog, then

R+360 analog+B, then R+360 analog+B+Z in a specific timing, really making me feel rewarded when I pulled it off.

I'll never forget pulling off the first 1080 in our group of friends and having them cheer me on. The fact that I felt so rewarded and had a group of friends cheering me on just for pulling off a move in a digital simulation is a testament to *1080° Snowboarding*. And of course, what game would be complete without unlockables? I remember staring intensely at the practice mode screen, reading the words "front flip" and "backflip" over and over, wondering "HOW DO I UNLOCK THESE TRICKS!" only to find out years later that they were only available to an unlockable secret character.

1080 is a must play for anyone looking to get a feel of the Nintendo 64 era. The physics are incredibly tight, the soundtrack is gritty, and the diverse characters are appealing with names that were oh so 90s. Dion Blaster anyone? *1080° Snowboarding* was a winter playground that I played over and over and over again and it can still be enjoyed to this day.

BUCK BUMBLE
(1998)

In *Buck Bumble* you play a cybernetic bumblebee
tasked with defeating mutated insects hell-bent
on assimilating everything in the garden... they're
called The Borg...no wait. Sorry...The Herd... *Buck
Bumble* is 20 or so levels of fairly straightforward
gameplay. Fly around their area, destroy the shit out
of anything you see, most of the time you need to
destroy some sort of Herd equipment. For the most
part, the single-player campaign is pretty average
as games of the time go. It was clearly rushed to be
released in time for Christmas. One look at the draw
distance will tell you that. However, *Buck Bumble* is
a guilty pleasure of mine for two reasons. One, the
disturbingly catchy theme song.

Open your mind's ears and let me hit you with the first experience you get with *Buck Bumble*. Fire up the cartridge and you're greeted with a bass-thumping club theme song dedicated to our insect protagonist. Here's the first few lyrics: "Right about now it's time to rock with the biggity Buck Bumble."

Seriously, do me a favor. Head to the Internet and look up the theme to *Buck Bumble*, then let it play as you read the rest of this entry. The second reason is an afterthought minigame in *Buck's* multiplayer called Buzz Ball. What is Buzz Ball, you ask? Well, you and a friend each control a Buck of your own on a gigantic man-sized soccer field. Your task is to use your weapons to blast the titanic soccer ball into your enemy's goal. You can pick up gun upgrades to send the ball flying even faster, or take out your opponent to try and score a goal while they're incapacitated.

My friends and I spent an absurd amount of time playing such a simple game, but we loved it. Hey *Rocket League*, *Buck Bumble* did it first!

CONKER'S BAD FUR DAY (2001)

From the moment I first picked up the box for *Conker's Bad Fur Day*, I knew it was something special. Rated Mature and plastered with warning labels, I had to find out what the seemingly innocent squirrel I first saw in *Diddy Kong Racing* was up to. And oh man, was I hooked from the first moment. Here's the premise; after a night of drunken debauchery, you wake up in a field with a wicked hangover and your goal is to get home. However, Conker's journey home is laden with trials and tribulations, from storming the beaches *Saving Private Ryan*-style to taking on a gigantic mechanized hay Terminator all while the evil Panther King is trying to catch you and use you as a replacement table leg. Sound ridiculous?

It is, and I loved every moment of it. *Conker's BFD* is bursting at the seams with comedy and pop culture references, and there's even a dash of drama. The characters are memorable, the platforming and boss fights are varied and fun, and the whole time you're treated to the witty dialog of Conker.

Oh, and did I mention the amazing multiplayer? Not only are you treated with a hilarious and amazing single-player, but you and up to three other friends can enjoy some awesome multiplayer with plenty of modes. Whether you're blasting the heads off some maniacal teddy bears, called "Teddies," with a sniper rifle, pulling off a weasel bank heist, or trying to steal and scramble the prehistoric eggs of a raptor, the multiplayer in *Conker's Bad Fur Day* is one of most fun on the 64 and that's saying something.

All in all, *Conker's Bad Fur Day* is a lowbrow love letter to pop culture and video games. It's a game that doesn't take itself too seriously and has a hilarious single-player, great mechanics, and a multiplayer that you can enjoy over and over. This game is a MUST PLAY for any gamer that enjoys fun and hey, isn't that what video games are all about?

DIDDY KONG RACING (1997)

How do you follow in the footsteps of *Mario Kart 64*? You take its fundamentals, slap on another popular Nintendo franchise, and take the competition to land, air, and sea! That is *Diddy Kong Racing*. Whether you're driving on the ground, flying through the sky blasting missiles, or hovering across a lagoon, *DKR* is a fast-paced kart race full of close calls, explosions, and sweet victory. But it didn't start that way. *Diddy Kong Racing* was originally developed as a Real Time Strategy game that later morphed into a racer headlining Timber the Tiger as the game's mascot. However, Nintendo offered up Diddy Kong and Rare snatched the opportunity.

Thus, *Diddy Kong Racing* was born. One of the things that immediately stands out about *Diddy Kong Racing* is its interactive menu. Once you're in the game you speak to the genie of the island, a big blue elephant that rides around on a flying carpet and speaks to you in a stereotypical Indian accent, and he allows you to switch between car, plane, or hovercraft. Once you've made your selection you're free to explore the island, checking out where the levels are and collecting hidden balloons.

The balloons are important. Each level requires you to have a certain amount of balloons before you can play it and the only way to get them is by exploring the over-world or completing races. Fans of *Banjo-Kazooie* will absolutely love and recognize this mechanic. Each level also contains shortcuts and even some hidden keys that allow you to access other portions of the over-world. This adds a nice level of charm to a game that could just simply have you select levels from a single screen. What still impresses me to this day is the creativity and polish *DKR* has. I mean, Rare could have easily kept this game to the basic racing and battle elements, but oh no – that wasn't enough for them.

First off, the weapons in the game were designated by colored balloons. Red for rockets, blue for boost, etc. If you collected multiple of the same balloons your reward would be upgraded. Plus, Rare added in special boss races to each world, where players took on everything from a giant stegosaurus to the final boss, a rocket-riding pig wizard named "Wizpig." Speaking of which, the characters in *DKR* definitely stood out. In fact, *Diddy Kong Racing* introduced us to some characters that would go on to become pillar Rare franchises. Conker and Banjo ring any bells? And of course there's a multiplayer where you can take on your friends in races or battles on land, air, or sea.

Diddy Kong Racing is a game where in every upbeat moment you can feel the love and attention to detail the developers put into this game.

GOLDENEYE 007 (1997)

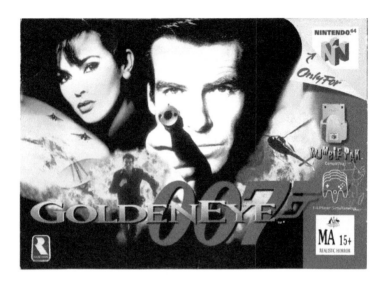

Words cannot express the excitement I felt awaiting the release of *GoldenEye 007*. I quickly scanned every current issue of *Nintendo Power* for details. Why? Because for me, it was my first chance to experience James Bond. See, my mom would never let me watch the James Bond movies due to the way they represented women. So, I would always get flak from my friends, and they'd talk about how cool Bond was and rub it in that I was missing out. But the video game was my chance to get the story of *GoldenEye* and get to know James Bond. Let me tell you, it was a wonderful way to experience it.

I vividly remember firing up the game, loading up the dam mission, and stepping into the shoes of

70

James Bond. This game had it all: huge arsenals of weapons from proximity mines to the rapid-fire assault rifles, spy gadgets, dramatic scenes like bungee jumping off the side of a dam, and plot twists. I first experienced the Trevelyan betrayal in the game and it blew my mind! This game had polish. Everything was Bond-themed, from save files being top secret files to missions selected on rolls of spy film. Even the pause menu was Bond's high tech spy watch. I spent countless hours replaying all the story missions on all difficulties, not just for the challenge but also to unlock cheat code modifiers.

Like paintball mode, where all the bullets are replaced by, well, paintballs, or DK mode, which gave you a giant head and long arms like Donkey Kong, both of were a blast in multiplayer. Oh man, the multiplayer! I could write this entire entry solely on the amazing multiplayer. While the single-player brought me an amazing experience, the multiplayer kept me playing *GoldenEye* for YEARS to come. With multiple game modes, tons of unlockable characters, and plenty of maps taken from the single-player, my friends and I began an after-school ritual of throwing down in *GoldenEye*. This game popularized first person shooters on console; in fact, I still invert my analog stick in modern shooters because that's the way it naturally was in *GoldenEye*.

So every time I'm playing a game today and have to change that setting, I get a little nostalgic reminder of one of the most legendary video games of all time.

MARIO PARTY
(1998)

I remember being skeptical when I first heard of *Mario Party*, thinking it was some new kiddie Mario game akin to *Mario is Missing*. However, what I received blew me away! The premise is simple. Mario and friends are sitting around debating who would make the best "Superstar." In order to find out once and for all, Toad suggests that the gang go on an adventure and whoever comes out on top will be declared the Superstar. So, as a player you get to pick your favorite Mario character and team up against friends or the CPU in one of the virtual Mario-themed game boards. The higher the dice roll, the further you go on the board, and landing on colored squares will either add or subtract coins. At the end of everyone's turn, players are tossed into a competition in one of 56 minigames.

The winner is rewarded with coins. The goal is to loop the board for a specified number of turns, attempting to buy as many stars as you can.

At the end of the game, the player with the most stars wins. There ares also items you can get to influence your dice rolls or ward off something bad. Speaking of which, in the spirit of friendly competition Bowser pops in to shake things up, and there's a Boo space that will allow you to spend your coins to steal coins or even a star from another player. When I landed on a Boo I could literally feel the power over my friends, watching and laughing as they begged and bartered, imploring me to steal a star from anyone but them. But the things that make this game so much fun to play over and over are the minigames. They're varied, sometimes making you team up with your opponents or incentivizing you to be the last man standing. Each one has their own unique charm, whether it's knocking your opponents into the ocean with a giant inflatable ball or picking them up in a giant crane game. It was like getting more than 50 games in one! And the competition was intense.

There were times when a minigame required me to spin the analog stick in circles as fast as I could and I ended up rubbing a hole through the skin in my hand! Fun fact: Nintendo actually received a few complaints about this and ended up sending gloves to those who complained. But injury or no, it was worth it for the satisfaction of defeating my opponents and gaining coins that might just allow me to pick up that next star. *Mario Party* is the Monopoly of the video game era. It's a happy and friendly premise that somehow turns darker the longer you play it and the more you feel invested. If you've ever wished for a test to determine how strong of a friendship you have with a person, look no further than *Mario Party*.

RUSH 2: EXTREME RACING USA

(1998)

When you hear of Midway's *Rush* franchise you probably instantly think of *San Francisco Rush* or *Rush 2049*. However, when I reminisce about the Rush racing franchise I think *Rush 2: Extreme Racing USA*. Now don't get me wrong, I loved throwing quarter after quarter into the *San Francisco Rush* arcade, but *Rush 2* for the N64 was the game that really clicked with me. First off, no longer are you racing the streets of San Francisco. In *Rush 2* you're taking the races to landmarks across the USA.

Las Vegas, New York, and Hawaii were the settings for high-octane console racing. The tracks were diversified and each had their own unique charm and bass-thumping music. Each level had its own hidden shortcuts, which you could use to cut ahead of your opponents and hit that next checkpoint before you ran out of time. There were a bunch of cars to choose from, and you could customize them with your own colors and racing stripes. However, hitting guard rails or other racers would damage the cosmetics of your vehicle, sometimes so much it was a wonder that this hunk of metal was still racing. Take too much damage and BOOM! You explode in a torrent of fire!

The racing was fun and did a good job expanding upon its predecessor, but the absolute best thing in this game is the Stunt track! Essentially, they turned players loose in a gigantic skate park made for cars! You could go solo or head-to-head against a friend to rack up as many points as possible by spinning or flipping your car without blowing up. I'm going to let you in on a little secret as to how to make Stunt Mode infinitely more enjoyable. Turn on the invincibility code and select the pickup truck! Now you're able to slam into anything full speed and send your car careening through the air in a series of insane flips and spins without worrying about things like exploding.

I can't even tell you how many countless hours my friends and I spent on the stunt course! I even found a glitch where if I hit the edge of the wall at max speed it would send my car high into the air in a series of quick front flips, allowing me to get over the wall of the course and continue my tricks falling outside of the level! This was a great way to rack up additional points and one of my friends always wanted to know how exactly I did it. Speaking of codes, *Rush 2* had a ton, from turning your car invisible to summoning killer rats. While *Rush 2: Extreme Racing USA* may not be one of the most popular games in the franchise it'll always have a place in my heart and childhood.

CRAIG

Craig is the founder of ScrewAttack and creator of
the original *Video Game Vault* series. Craig credits
the *Video Game Vault* series as playing a huge part in
ScrewAttack's early success and helping expose an
entire generation of viewers to games they may have
never heard of otherwise. He loves the Vault so much,
he decided ScrewAttack should write a book about it.

@StutteringCraig

CRUIS'N USA
(1996)

One of the most amazing things about the N64 was the promise it showed to gamers that "the arcades were coming home." The idea of being able to play games that were just as good as the arcade version was mind-boggling. On the SNES we had some solid arcade ports like *Street Fighter 2* and *Killer Instinct* but nothing that really felt EXACTLY like the arcade. *Cruis'n USA* was one of the first games I remember seeing and saying "Wow, it's JUST like the arcade!" Having graphics that good on a home video game system was amazing. It seemed like everything was in the N64 game that was in the arcade: secret cars like the cop car and school bus, quarter-sucking difficulty, and of course, hot girls in bikinis. The only thing that was missing was the steering wheel!

The second you turn on the game you're greeted with some amazingly cheesy music that was built to stick out in the arcades.... "CRUUUUUIS'N YEAH! ...... *CRUIS'N USA!*" It rings like a mid-90s symphony in my head. Beautiful. Just beautiful.

Speaking of beauty, one of the most amazing things about the game was how they used the shitty N64 draw distance (what you could see coming in front of you) to its advantage. You couldn't tell what was coming up next, so when something like the Golden Gate Bridge popped up, it was actually kind of awe-inspiring. It was exciting to see what was coming next. As you make your way across the United States blistering through towns and countryside you quickly realize that you are hitting some crazy speeds, more than 140 MPH consistently, which makes it even more amazing when you casually slam headfirst into a semi.

You would think that all parties involved would be killed immediately, but you know what? That's the joy of arcade racing games! You just keep on going and burst through the next barricade in hopes of getting a Top 10 time so you can put your initials on a license plate.

MARIO KART 64 (1997)

Look, if you owned an N64, there's a 97.2% chance that you also owned *Mario Kart 64*. There are literally no stats to back that statement up but judging by the few buddies I had growing up, I'm pretty sure that's accurate. You didn't have to be a hardcore gamer to be into what *Mario Kart* was bringing to your N64. At the end of the day, it was all about good ol' fashioned fun.

The beautiful thing about *MK64* is the diversity of the game and its levels. You can be racing on the beach, on the farm, in the desert...and that's just in the Mushroom Cup! It goes without saying that this stands up well today because when we pop it in at the ScrewAttack HQ and get a few rounds in, the mood is intense, there's always lots of laughs, and there's always that state of exhilaration when someone hits a shortcut on Koopa Troopa Beach or Rainbow Road. It's a well-known fact that you can ask 100 people who have played *Mario Kart 64*, and pretty much all of them will have a different favorite level or, if you were to bring up a certain level, they would say "OH! I LOVE THAT LEVEL!"

Sure, everyone knew that guy who was just ridiculously better than everyone else, but for the most part, anyone and everyone could hold their own in a race. Why? The two most broken words in the English language: blue shell. Since its inception in *Mario Kart 64*, the blue shell has gone on to cause more heartache in video games than Pizza Pockets, but at the end of the day, just like Pizza Pockets, it's oh so delicious to deliver a hit of the blue shell to the leader of a race. What's amazing is that some people say *Mario Kart 64*'s Battle Mode is the pinnacle of the series.

This is a game that was released in the mid-90s and people are STILL arguing about who the best is in battle mode. We're talking four players at the same time, green shells flying around, red shells coming up on your tailpipe, fake question blocks, banana peels... whew... it was and still is insanity. There's a reason *Mario Kart 64* sold the second most games on the N64. It's amazing.

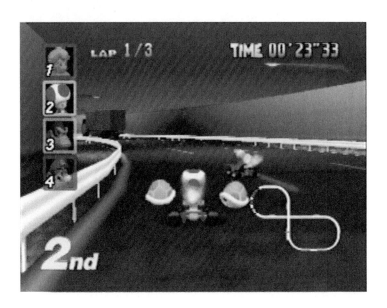

NBA HANGTIME

(1997)

I realize that a lot of people reading this book probably
have NO idea what *NBA Hangtime* is. That's cool, but
I suggest you get to know it. I am a huge fan of *NBA
Jam*. LOVE IT! For me, it was a game that changed how
I looked at video games. While *NBA Hangtime* may not
have the *Jam* name attached to it, it may be one of the
best games in the series. So many things were added
to the series in *Hangtime* that were considered staples,
yet so many people forget about this game.

It's kind of like how people forget that Mega Man's
Mega Buster Charge Shot first appeared in the
overlooked *Mega Man 4*. So what was added in
Hangtime? The spin move that allowed you to escape
people shoving you, alley-oops, and double dunks that

allow your team to catch fire if you hit three in a row. But the biggest addition is definitely customizable characters. This is where *Hangtime* totally shines.

You can customize your player to be a giant wolf, a tiny wizard, look like Scottie Pippen, and anything else in between. Then you can take it a step further and customize your player to your play style. Like to shoot threes? You could bump up your shooting ability. Want to dunk all over people? Fill up the dunk attribute. It's amazing. The detail attached to the player customization is where I really saw the power of what the N64 could do. *NBA Jam* on the SNES and Genesis couldn't handle unique player faces, but on the 64 players actually looked like they should in real life. It was the next level of graphics at the time and it blew my fragile little mind. Legitimately, one of my favorite things to do with the guys at the ScrewAttack HQ is play a four-player game of *Hangtime* where we all use our created characters. It's so much fun. Even if you're a casual basketball fan, *Hangtime* is one of those games that once you pick it up, it's impossible to put down. Truly one of my all-time favorites.

NFL BLITZ 2000 (1999)

NFL Blitz 2000 is a game that couldn't be made in today's over-politically correct, worried about public perception world. Take the fact that there's a concussion epidemic in professional football today and that *Blitz* is built around glorifying the violence and nope...just nope. Let me break it down for you: *NFL Blitz 2000* is the best American football game ever made. It's incredibly fast-paced, easy to play yet hard to master, and filled to the brim with secret codes. Everything about *Blitz* is over the top, even down to the cursing announcer (Tim Kitzrow). Now the N64's technology was obviously inferior to the arcade, but the N64 had something the arcade couldn't offer: the Rumble Pack.

The Rumble Pack was a device you attached to the back of your N64 controller that allowed you to "feel" the impact of the game. When you take that rumble technology and pair it with one of *NFL Blitz's* most memorable feature—tackling after the referee called the play over—you have yourself a winner. While a lot of people remember the late hits, *NFL Blitz 2000* really stands on its own by being a fast-paced, high-scoring game that allows those with skills to excel and those who suck to suck.

Anyone who follows ScrewAttack closely knows that Shaun Bolen and I have an EPIC *NFL Blitz* rivalry that continues to this day. Unfortunately that rivalry is incredibly one-sided with me getting the better of Bolen 95 percent of the time we play, but even then it's incredibly fun. Bolen has been able to go from complete crap in the game, losing to me constantly to actually beating me.

That's *NFL Blitz* in a nutshell: easy to play but hard to master. Isn't that the key to all good games? Remember how I said a game like *NFL Blitz* couldn't work in today's world? Well Electronic Arts, now the holder of the *NFL Blitz* trademark, tried to reboot *Blitz* a few years ago. In theory this sounded great, but after the reboot came out it was nerfed with no late hits, wonky gameplay, and just a different feel than what made the original so great. What a shame. With that said, it's always good to appreciate what you have at the time and never take it for granted. *NFL Blitz 2000* is an amazing example of that.

YOSHI'S STORY
(1998)

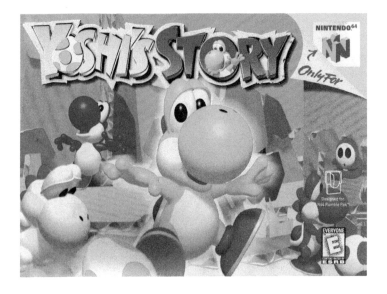

When you look at the box art of *Yoshi's Story* you see bright, beautiful colors. I mean, this legitimately is one of the cutest games on the N64 with one of the most unique looks. The problem with this is that all the cuteness is just a cover for the bed of lies this game lies in.

What the game tells you is that a bunch of Yoshis are out to recover the Super Happy Tree. On your way, you play through fairly unique levels while using your giant tongue to eat fruit...lots of fruit. But what I see is a bunch of drugged-up dinos out to recover the goods so they can keep getting their kicks. How else would you explain the drug dog Poochie who helps you find the fruit and the way the Yoshis trip balls when you get the last fruit. You will have never seen a dinosaur have an orgasm prior to *Yoshi's Story*, but once you see the face of Yoshi after collecting that last fruit it will be stained into your brain.

With technology advancing so quickly I realize that some of you reading this may have never actually used a chalkboard before. Prior to the Internet, in school we actually had to write things on a chalkboard with real chalk. The only reason I bring this up is because one of the worst things you can do as a person in this world is drag fingernails down a chalkboard. It makes the most horrific sound in the world – similar to the sound made when all the Yoshis sing together. Some people would say that having six high-pitched dinosaurs singing a happy song at once is incredibly cute. I say I'd like to rip my ears off and cover the holes with rubber cement so I don't ever have to hear it again.

Now I realize that what I'm telling you may sound like I don't like *Yoshi's Story*. That couldn't be further from the truth. It's an AMAZING game that is incredibly unique. What I don't like about it is that it's CLEARLY a metaphor that embraces drug culture with Yoshis representing addicts and fruit representing drugs.

Yeah, try getting that out of your head next time you play it.

NICK

Nick has been a personality, editor, and writer for lots of ScrewAttack shows since he became a part of the crew in 2008. Gaming has been in his blood since the day he was born, with some of his most treasured video game memories stemming from Nintendo's 64-bit wonder.

@THENervousNick

BANJO-KAZOOIE (1998)

If there's one thing that was totally synonymous with the N64 in my mind, it was 3-D platformers. What *Super Mario 64* pioneered, every single other company tried to replicate. How successful they were depends on how much you love games like *Gex*...or *Glover*...Okay, let's be real, most of them are lucky to have aged with any grace at all. But leave it to a studio in the UK called Rare to take seemingly any genre and make something beyond your wildest expectations.

That's what *Banjo-Kazooie* did for 3-D platforming. This game is made of that real video game stuff. The vibrant graphics, the tight controls, the infectious music, the characters brimming with personality, the large worlds to explore, the hilarious and distinctly

British wit; put simply, *Banjo-Kazooie* is unmistakably Rare. It has this children's storybooklike plot in which a bear named Banjo and a bird named Kazooie, who lives in his backpack, set off to rescue Banjo's sister from an evil witch who wants to suck out her beauty with a machine.

Along the way, this mole named Bottles teaches you new moves and abilities (which was always one of my favorite parts of the game) to help you reach areas you couldn't before or defeat enemies who used to be too powerful so that you can collect puzzle pieces to open up new levels. Who comes up with this stuff? Rare did.

And it's freakin' beautiful. Lesser platformers from this era might get a pass on their crude graphics or design choices simply because they were exploring a new frontier in gaming. *Banjo-Kazooie* needs no such forgiveness; even in the modern age, it's still platforming heaven.

THE LEGEND OF ZELDA: MAJORA'S MASK (2000)

No game made of 75 percent recycled assets and pushed out in a single year has any right to be as good as *The Legend of Zelda: Majora's Mask* turned out. And yet, the end result turned out to be one of my personal favorite games ever made. Funny how that works out sometimes, isn't it?

In comparison to its predecessor, the N64 golden child *Ocarina of Time*, *Majora's Mask* is nowhere NEAR as inviting. From its unsettling music and locations, to its dark themes of loss and death, to the way you wear masks to transform into deceased heroes and console their loved ones...oh yeah, and that giant falling moon with the face of a murderer that will crush the world in three days, this is a game that carries an increasing sense of dread from start to finish. As the hero, you must repeatedly live through these final days until you acquire the means to stop the moon.

Cool!

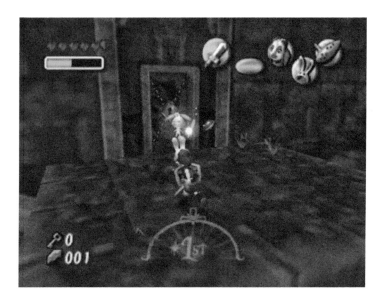

What's even cooler, though, is that this gives you the chance to see how every NPC chooses to live out their final days. Everybody is a fully fleshed-out character, not just a body to fill up space. There's even this awesome theory that the residents in each of Termina's major locations embody the different stages of grief. Needless to say, this is easily one of the more emotional Zelda games out there. It's a thing of beauty. It's this emotional throughline that puts

Majora's Mask above all other Zelda games in my book, even if the game can be mechanically more frustrating than its *Ocarina of Time* ancestor. You want to stop this moon, and not just to say you completed another game; you want to so that all of these stories have happy endings. For real, though, why does the moon have to have that face??

KIRBY 64: THE CRYSTAL SHARDS (2000)

The speed at which information moves today is so much faster than it was just in the year 2000. Today, between all the trailers and gameplay that gets posted online, I feel like I have real reasons to justify my excitement for a game. Back in those days, we mostly just went off of a hunch. Based off of one such hunch, I ordered *Kirby 64: The Crystal Shards* online and couldn't think about anything else until the day it arrived. Now, even back then, I had been wrong about being excited for a game before.

This was not one of those times. Kirby dared to keep the playing field 2-D when everyone else was trying to force their characters into 3-D planes. But what really made this game amazing was being able to copy enemy powers like in previous games and then combine them with others for countless combinations to discover. This was the feature I bought this game for. With the cutter power mixed in with some electricity, you got a Darth Maul-style double-edged light saber.

Double up on rock powers and you become a thundering golem. Combine bombs with ice powers and you get an explosive snowman. Or merge ice with electricity instead and Kirby becomes a refrigerator that launches food as projectiles of death! I could have spent hours trying combinations I hadn't thought of yet. In fact... I did.

BLAST CORPS
(1997)

The beauty of the *Video Game Vault* is that you can either revisit an old favorite or discover a new one. As much as I've always loved Rare, there were some games I'd never experienced until recent years. Among them: *Blast Corps.*, a game that I swear was made just for me. See, there's this running gag at ScrewAttack that I break everything I touch, and in *Blast Corps.*, destruction is the primary objective. In each level, you clear a path for a slow-moving nuclear missile carrier by tearing down everything in the way using whichever vehicles the mission requires.

Bulldozers can flatten farm sheds, dump trucks do donuts through apartments with people still living inside them, mech suits stomp skyscrapers into dust from the top down...and a motorcycle fires missiles. I'm convinced that demolition has never been as satisfying in any game as it was in *Blast Corps*. The sound effects have impact, the game sometimes shows you the property damage you cause in dollar amounts, and everything explodes. No matter what it is. Oh, Rare...you're just trying to impress me.

SAM

Sam Mitchell has been playing games since he could walk. From 1988 until now, gaming has been the cornerstone of his life. Joining ScrewAttack in 2012, he has added his bold opinion to everything he can get his hands on. Also his mom thinks he is really handsome.

@ScrewAttackSam

DONKEY KONG 64 (1999)

Donkey Kong 64 was one of the most highly anticipated games I can remember from my childhood; after all, it was the last great Nintendo franchise to make the jump to 3-D. Luckily, our anticipation wasn't unwarranted; *DK64* was just about everything you could ask for in a 3-D Donkey Kong game. Sure it had problems, like everything being character-specific (blueprints, balloons, pads, buttons, weapons, even bananas) but it also had amazing platforming, great bosses, and a gargantuan amount of secrets to discover. It might not live up to *Mario 64* or *Banjo-Kazooie* on gameplay alone, but it's unforgettable to me because of how I acquired the game.

As a wee, baby child at the tender age of eleven, I was young, innocent, and full of hope. I hoped that *Donkey Kong 64* would do as much 3-D justice to its predecessors as *Mario 64* did. I remember it clearly, November 1999. It was a few days after Thanksgiving, and I was on holiday break, morose over the fact that I would have to wait a whole month until I got *DK64* for Xmas. Little did I know, my parents had secretly purchased the game for me and had placed the cartridge in my Nintendo 64. They had planted a landmine of childish joy, and I was about to stumble upon it. That day was an excellent day.

Playing the game, I remember being astonished by the immense size of the *DK64's* world. It had tons of levels, an entire Kong family to play as, and to tie it all together, a timeless rap song. "But why shouldn't it be this big?" I thought to myself. After all this game was so cutting edge and amazing that it required a

RAM expansion for the aging 64 to even play it. This is truly a time to be alive! The game was a complete blast and offered little me at least 60 hours of swinging on vines, pounding crocs, collecting golden bananas, and even getting the high score on the original *Donkey Kong* arcade cabinet inside the game. *DK64* was my life for that holiday break.

I have a vivid memory of sitting cross-legged on a shaggy, beige carpet in my small room. The lights off, the warm glow of a CRT monitor illuminating my face. I was about 2 hours in before I realized that in my haste to begin my adventure I had not even stopped to look at the menu options, so I decided to take a peek. There it was, in big banana font letters: "Multiplayer." I was blown away, my mouth silently forming the words my brain was thinking..... "Holy shit." This game has everything. The multiplayer, consisting of some sort of strange four-player monkey military simulator, wasn't the highlight of the game, but it was just about the sweetest cherry on top that you could imagine.

F-ZERO X (1998)

You know what's awesome? Speed! Oh, and an intergalactic, insanely dangerous, space derby racing league! Few games have ever captured the essence of awesome like *F-Zero X* did, and it wasn't just its insanely awesome world full of aliens and high-stakes space races; you could have re-skinned the game with Volvos being driven by Ben Stein and it still would have been one of the highest-octane experiences available on the N64.

Now, the first *F-Zero* on SNES was already good, but *F-Zero X* kicked everything up a notch. The gameplay was like riding a Ducati through the stampede in *The Lion King*. The music is so badass that it deserves a parental warning sticker, and it doesn't even have lyrics. The graphics are said to be coded by the ghost of Bruce Lee and a dragon who changed his name to Big Blue (despite being red) after listening to the game's soundtrack. In fact, *F-Zero X* is one of the only N64 games that runs at a solid 60 FPS, which was nearly unheard of for its time. There are no experiences on the N64 that feel quite like trading paint with a giant slug monster at 800 KPH while you fly through a series of turns and tunnels on a race track that can only be described as an industrial Leviathan.

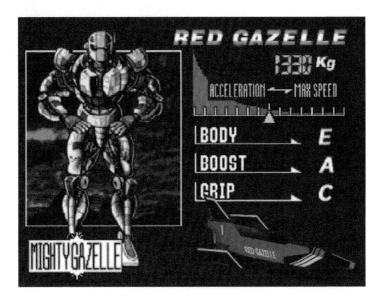

Not only is the racing top-notch and light years ahead of its time, the game also has a surprising amount of customization and replayability for its era. *F-Zero X* is adrenaline in the form of a video game. In fact, the word "awesome" fails in describing *F-Zero X* – the word "awesome" aspires to be like *F-Zero X* when it grows up. If I were to walk out my door tomorrow and see an army of righteous bear soldiers strapping jetpacks to their furry backs and flying into the sky to fight a flock of Nazi vultures, I would stop and look on in awe because something was almost as badass as *F-Zero X*.

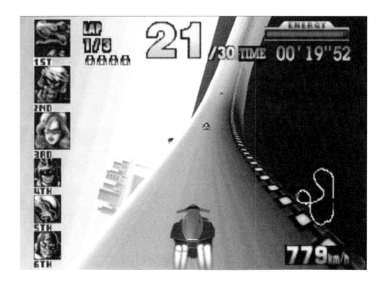

HARVEST MOON 64 (1999)

Like pretty much every kid in the 90s, I had a firm opinion on things like chores and tedious manual labor: it all sucked hard and I didn't want to do any of it. If you had told me at the age of twelve that my grandfather had passed away and left me his farm and now it was my responsibility to take care of the homestead, I would have said, "screw that," and run off to play some N64. Ironically, the game I would have been playing at that time happens to be about inheriting your dead grandpa's farm and doing a bunch of boring shit for like...a hundred hours.

Harvest Moon 64 might as well have been named *Boring Rural Life Simulator 64*. Honestly, this game has absolutely no right to be as addictive as it is, but here we are, reading about it in a book because it's so damn good.

You look like you want to say something.

Video games are a weird medium, and this is highlighted by the fact that games like *Harvest Moon 64* not only exist, but are almost universally loved. Now you could make an argument that it is great because of its core gameplay, which revolves around getting your farm to be a profitable establishment via growing plants, chopping trees, brushing your livestock... ya' know, farmer stuff. You could also argue that the village of Flower Bug is bursting at the seams with funny, interesting townsfolk, or that the seasonal events and festivals keep gameplay fresh. While all these arguments hold water, the real reason *Harvest Moon 64* is so good is because it's one of the most accurate dating simulators ever.

Now you might think I'm pulling your leg, but trust me, I'm not. In *Harvest Moon*, getting the girl isn't as easy as saying, "I choose you," and then talking to her once a day, hell no. Much like real life, *Harvest Moon*'s dating requires a keen sense of time management. Not making money? Not on top of your daily errands? Well, too bad. No girl for you, bozo! Hell, it doesn't stop there either; even if you get married, it's still difficult to keep her happy. You have a handful of extra-busy days on the farm and you just don't have time to spend with your betrothed? That hussy is out of there and back to living with her parents in no time. That's life: spend too much time shearing sheep, and you're suddenly divorced.

Now as an adult, weathered by the harsh winds of life, I look back on *Harvest Moon 64* fondly, but I don't look back on it with a gleeful smile. I look back with a knowing nod, silently thanking it for preparing me for the cruel realities of what it takes to juggle love and life.

JET FORCE GEMINI (1999)

LISTEN UP, WORMS AND GERMS! Today is the first day in your new life as the commander of two Jet Force soldiers and a weaponized space war dog. You will do this from a third-person perspective and you will lead your team to victory against the evil insect tyrant, Mizar. Yes, I can assure you that this is as badass as it sounds! However, do not for one second think that this will be easy. The task ahead of you will not only require you to be extremely fluent with a controller that is now dated and mediocre, it will also require you to not smash that old, creaky, plastic bastard straight through your TV.

Your mission will be to take the aforementioned ragtag group of playable characters through a gauntlet of ant-based alien scum. You will rain hellfire down on your insect enemies with an arsenal full of weapons that includes plasma shotguns, tri-rocket launchers, and, of course, the infamous Shocker! Don't forget, you will be using many of these weapons from the back of an adorable, militarized space pouch. As you rampage through the opposing insect army, try to save as many tiny teddy bear people as you can too. Despite the similarities of these fuzzy creatures, I assure you they are not Ewoks from *Star Wars*, and they by no means infringe on any copyright laws.

Fear not, if the single-player campaign is too daunting, which it most likely is seeing as it is easily regarded as one of the hardest N64 games ever made, *Jet Force Gemini* contains one of the most stellar combat-based multiplayer modes you can find on the N64. On top of its excellent multiplayer, Rare went the extra mile when making this game by jamming it full of secrets. There is a laundry list of unlockable characters for multiplayer, as well as different stages and modes, but one secret in particular takes the cake in my book.

If you are clever enough to find the secret ant arcade and also have the tokens required to play *Jeff & Barry Racing 1* and *2*, you will be treated to a clone of a classic NES game developed by Rare by the name of *R.C. Pro-Am*. Now as cool as that may be, it gets better. Achieve the high score on both these arcades and you will unlock a secret 3-D racer multiplayer mode. This 3-D racing mode is a clone of another Rare game by the name of *Diddy Kong Racing*. It is for all of above reasons that *Jet Force Gemini* will go down in history as one of the most badass games to ever grace the 64.

PILOTWINGS 64
(1996)

Have you ever wanted to go through the process of getting your pilot's license without actually getting a pilot's license? No you haven't. No one ever has. That's probably why I was so blown away by *Pilotwings 64* when I first played it at my neighbor's house as a child. Hear me out, I was about nine at the time, and I was under the impression that tutorials were probably the worst parts of video games. Just shut up and let me play the damn game! Seeing how *Pilotwings 64* was about 90 percent tutorials, I just wasn't a fan at that age. Luckily I took a second look at *Pilotwings 64* later in life, during my teens.

Apparently something had changed — flying a gyrocopter through hoops, hang gliding through air drafts, I was suddenly addicted. The beauty of *Pilotwings 64* lies in its construction: its bones consist of its impressively competent flight sim gameplay, and on those bones they built an insanely addictive, arcade-style point system and dressed it up with a fun and approachable cartoonish graphic style. The final structure presented to consumers is a game unlike any other experience on the 64.

As a launch title for the N64, *Pilotwings* was meant to show off what the new console could do in terms of graphics. Let me tell you, for its time, it achieved that goal and then some, but many people were more surprised by the fact that it was more than a tech demo – it was a great game, too! Offering a cast of pilots to choose from, all with individual characteristics, four different "vehicles" to fly, and one of the smoothest learning curves in gaming, it was no surprise why it succeeded, even if it took me a few years of growing up to see it.

Pilotwings 64 taught me one thing as a young, budding gamer: a challenge can be more than completing a difficult task. A challenge can be mastering a simple task. Sure, it's satisfying to just make it through all the hoops and land, but to do it with enough grace and style to make it look easy is downright intoxicating.

SNOWBOARD KIDS (1998)

Snowboard Kids is a simple pleasure and a simple game. Not to say that it lacks depth, but it is pretty much exactly what it looks like – *Mario Kart* meets snowboarding. If you like *Mario Kart*, you'll like *Snowboard Kids*, because at their core they are essentially the same thing: race to the finish while using assorted power-ups and weapons scattered around the map. Luckily for us though, *Snowboard Kids* does have a few features that set it apart from other kart racers besides just going downhill in the snow.

In the late 90s, anything that could be classified as an "extreme sport" was hotter than mama's biscuits. Unlike *Mario Kart 64*, where you primarily stay glued to the ground, *Snowboard Kids* heavily featured jumps, ramps, cliffs—hell, just about anything that would give you an excuse to decouple from the earth and "catch some air," as the youth would put it. With this abundance of "air-catching" came a trick system, and despite it being rather simple, it stood out as one of the game's key features. The game even had a halfpipe track specifically designed for just doing tricks.

From its dick-nosed roster of playable characters, all with their own individual stats, to the fact that there are levels that don't even have snow (BOOM! Grassboard Kids – mind blowing!) *Snowboard Kids* never takes itself too seriously. The game's charming sense of humor is one of its strongest characteristics and kept the game focused on silly fun for up to four-players. The game also uniquely lacked a "go" button, seeing as how you are going downhill and acceleration isn't really an option. Whether you like it or not,

gravity is going to take you to the bottom of the
mountain, so try and stay upright and have some fun
on your way down.

Now you might be thinking, "Why play this over *Mario
Kart*?" Well, let me tell you: sabotage! Yes, nailing
someone in *Mario Kart* with a green shell is nice, but
there's something about *Snowboard Kids* that turns it
up a notch. When you're flying down the mountain and
you smack your friend in the back of the head with a
frying pan and he goes tumbling into the snow, it's just
devastating for them and all the more satisfying for
you...that is, until they get their revenge.

STAR WARS: ROGUE SQUADRON (1998)

Okay, let's face it, pretty much every person ever has watched the original *Star Wars* trilogy and thought to themselves, "Hot damn I would love to fly one of those spaceships." Well, *Star Wars: Rogue Squadron* let us do just that, and it was just as badass as we had all hoped. You play as Luke Skywalker leading a daring team of pilots into some of the most epic fights in *Star Wars* history. Want to fly an X-wing on Tatooine? Got it! Race over the ocean on Mon Cala, the home world of Admiral Ackbar, while screaming "IT'S A TRAP!"? Can do!

One thing *Rogue Squadron* knew it had to do, however, was keep its FPS high and stable, but even then the developers knew it wouldn't be enough. They needed higher resolution and they needed to be at the upper echelon of standard def. And thanks to the N64 RAM expansion they were able to do it. After upgrading your N64 with a mind blowing 4 MB of RAM, you were able to play in "high resolution mode," literally doubling the resolution to a whopping 640 x 480! Now that might not sound like much to you now, but it was a night and day difference back then!

Rogue Squadron was the kind of game that you could beat in a day, but it would take you ages to get to 100 percent. Despite only having 15 missions in the campaign, *Rogue Squadron* had a surprising amount of replayability in trying to achieve the gold medals in every level. To do that, you needed to customize all of your ships, including the A-, V-, Y-, and of course, X-wings, plus a snowspeeder! If the original five ships weren't enough to fill out your hanger, don't worry, *Rogue Squadron* had secret ships. Just type a few codes and soon you could fly in some of the most exotic ships in the galaxy like the TIE Interceptor, the Millennium Falcon, and even a Naboo starfighter that was so well hidden in the game that it wasn't discovered until six months after its launch! As cool as they were, none of those ships beat my personal favorite, the 1969 Buick Electra. Yes, you read that correctly, you can take a Buick into combat against a fleet of imperial TIE fighters.

If all of this wasn't enough, the game had even more hidden secrets including stages like the Battle of Hoth and the destruction of the Death Star. There was even a secret mode where you could pilot an AT-ST! *Rogue*

Squadron found a way to capture the intensity of a real *Star Wars* dogfight that had never been seen before on consoles, and for that reason it still remains one of the best Star Wars games ever made.

SEAN

Sean Hinz is currently the Senior Manager of Operations over at ScrewAttack and has been in the video game industry since 2010. After a lifetime of playing video games, it's easy for Sean to reflect on his experience with Nintendo's first foray into the fifth generation of gaming consoles, via the Nintendo 64, and how it shaped his childhood.

@SeanHinz

GAUNTLET LEGENDS (1999)

Having a game that could really show off the power
of four controller ports was pretty important back in
the late 90s. There really weren't many consoles that
could do it without the need of a multitap, and even
then, most games that supported the option weren't
too great. But since the whole setup was native to
the device, Midway knew that a Nintendo 64 was the
perfect hardware for bringing the arcade juggernaut
that is *Gauntlet* to living rooms everywhere. Developed
in the mid-80s, *Gauntlet* was a fantasy themed hack-
n-slash arcade game that had players diving through a
massive number of dungeons as one of four characters.
While the formula is very much the same, *Gauntlet*

Legends sought to introduce the game to an entirely new generation of gamers.

Using the power of the polygon, Legends took the franchise into the third dimension for the first time ever, and nearly every aspect of the game received a graphical upgrade. I personally loved the face-melting power of the RAM Pak installed in my N64 expansion port for the best visual experience *Gauntlet Legends* had to offer. My friends and I would get together on the weekend as wizards, warriors, Valkyries, or archers and compete with each other to amass the most gold and kills in each world. Nothing could stop me from trolling those guys, stealing items from open chests using someone else's keys and creating enemy chokepoints along the Castle Armory. We'd even challenge each other to not eat food through an entire level and see who came out with the most health.

My buddy Matt was typically the elf and almost always the hungriest. If wailing on endless hordes of enemies with the "standard" attacks started to feel like a bore, the game offered up some insane power-ups, which could set enemies on fire, make me a giant, or give me super speed. The wealth of secret characters alongside the lack of any sort of level cap made *Gauntlet Legends* the best hack-n-slash on the N64, if not the best home consoles had ever seen.

I could play it for hundreds of hours, with three of my friends, and that's sort of what gaming is all about.

HYDRO THUNDER (2000)

Midway was the sort of publisher who excelled at bringing classic arcade experiences to home consoles, and *Hydro Thunder* shined on Nintendo's. It was a colorful roller coaster ride of awesome that challenged me and my friends in a race to finish in first place, while surviving blinding speed across dynamic levels. While it found its way to more than one platform, the N64 version was different from other home consoles by capitalizing on the four available controller ports – so long as you had the Expansion Pack of course.

In the vein of *Cruis'n USA* or even *Outrun*, *Hydro Thunder* is an arcade racer that puts you behind the wheel of an insane number of transforming boats. These boats were so insane that when you picked some of the higher-level options, the game would literally scream at you, "you're CRAZY!" as a sort of fire alarm screeched in the background. Tarzan screams as you dive off cliffs and crumble environments made for some nail-biting races, but my favorite part was the emphasis on speed. Red and blue boost icons littered the track, guiding you to explosive jumps and even a secret passage. Hitting a boost icon would make your boat transform as if it were preparing to blast right off the screen.

If you were good enough, you could boost the length of any track. Bringing a few friends along for the ride made for an even more competitive experience, because rubbing is racing, after all. After blasting through 13 tracks, I found that getting to the secret tracks and boats required taking first place in every track.

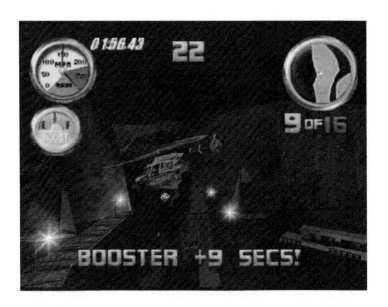

I definitely would pad out the end game, but I recall a friend of mine from school coming over and we worked all night to get past the Ship Graveyard by boosting through a secret waterfall. Not uncommon for a game like *Hydro Thunder*, but immensely satisfying every time. And every list has to have an extreme racing game with arcade roots.

TUROK: DINOSAUR HUNTER (1997)

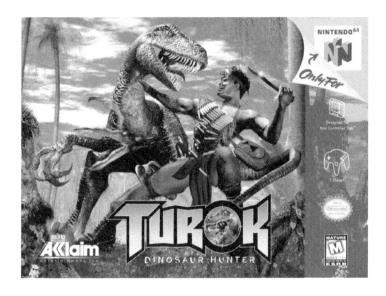

The advent of shooters wouldn't really come to form on home consoles for a few years, yet Nintendo still managed to blow my childish mind through the power of dinosaurs. Walking through a world where jungle cats roared in the distance constantly would put anyone on edge, but the silhouette of a raptor sprinting towards you out of the mist was terrifying! I remember vividly my first encounter, knife in hand, dying in a heap of sweat and panic. Then I realized I also had a tech bow in my inventory, and from that point forward all raptors would soon come to fear the name Turok.

Given the odd shape of the N64 controller, mechanically the game struck a balance between movement and the camera, thanks to the CPad and analog stick, respectively. This lent itself to the platforming, another ambitious part of the game, since most FPS at the time would barely touch the idea of having a camera hop around a level. I distinctly remember the first column section being placed specifically before the first save location. A fall wouldn't kill you, but the game certainly made you earn the right to make any sort of real progress. Levels were locked behind a series of elaborate keys and those would be my primary objective between killing pretty much anything. I should probably mention how much blood there is. For a Nintendo game, *Turok* was pretty gruesome. Every few death animations I'd catch an enemy in the neck and watch as he bled out right where he stood.

As you would get to the later levels you'd gain access to new and more powerful tech: particle accelerators, alien weapons, fusion cannons; no dinosaur was safe from the pain train that I was bringing down on them. Especially if you went back and turned a few classic cheats. Invincibility, unlimited ammo, big head mode! *Turok* was, like most classic games, in love with the idea of having fun. That's how you ended up with gunwielding cyborg dinosaurs, massive bosses, and a Native American protagonist on a quest to "make dinosaurs extinct. Again." Sure, games like *GoldenEye* and *Perfect Dark* offer up these memorable multiplayer moments with friends, but the story campaign can't touch the magical world of *Turok: Dinosaur Hunter*.

WAVE RACE 64
(1996)

Not since the 90s was the idea of racing Jet Skis considered "cool." In fact, that might not have actually ever been the case, but Nintendo thought it was and that's what led to the first party exclusive *Wave Race 64*.

Having the Kawasaki license meant that players could have exclusive access to the hottest water cars on waves. And for the time, the water physics were definitely pushing the boundaries on home consoles. The game was once quoted from Miyamoto himself as being able to use 80 percent of the console's power. For a launch title, that's a pretty insane feat.

In *Wave Race 64* there were four racers to choose from, with customizable Jet Skis. Each came with their own advantages and disadvantages. My friends and I used to play as D. Mariner as a sort of handicap. Dave was a bigger Jet Ski jockey, and trying to do anything other than jump a ramp in a straight line was a dangerous prospect. But anytime the tubby driver managed to actually execute a stunt, my sense of accomplishment would air throughout the room. That was especially the case when playing the stunt mode specifically, which challenged you to earn as many points as possible on a given track rather than battling the AI first. Sure it focused on racing through a series of rings, but it also taught me the finer paths for each track to make sure I was getting the best times, something that proved extremely useful in the Championship mode and Time Trial mode.

Still, my fondest moments were spent in the two-player split screen where you slalom through enough buoys to hit maximum power and blast past your friends for the finish line. The chill soundtrack, iconic announcer, and impressive visuals make *Wave Race 64* a beloved classic for Nintendo 64 owners. While it would lead to a lackluster sequel on the GameCube, nothing could really capture the magic of racing alongside dolphins in a Jet Ski or doing a barrel roll with a fat guy to prove to your friends what a badass you were like *Wave Race 64*.

WINBACK: COVERT OPERATIONS
(1999)

These days it seems like everyone loves covert-based shooters, but most gamers couldn't tell you the genre's origin. Pull back the curtain and sure enough you'll find the N64 exclusive *WinBack: Covert Operations*. Of course, most of the world has forgotten this game exists because of its awful name, but spend 10 minutes with it and you'll discover just why the genre is so awesome. JeanLuc Cougar, stealth spy extraordinaire, is a member of the organization S.C.A.T., tasked with protecting the world from a space-based laser satellite.

Wow, these guys are really bad at naming stuff...

So you need to complete your mission by sneaking around an enemy installation and using cover to get the tactical advantage over the "Crying Lions" goons. This idea of snapping to cover was just beginning to be explored by games like *Metal Gear Solid*, but *WinBack* chose to forgo most stealth options in favor of action. Explosive barrels and laser traps lined the sort-of linear combat areas, which helped pace the game out between firefights. While my pistol packed a punch and had unlimited ammo, the shotgun and submachine gun certainly had their place. Combine that with the occasional special weapon or C4 and there was nothing JeanLuc and I couldn't accomplish, minus the occasional death by cutscene or even getting stuck in the geometry.

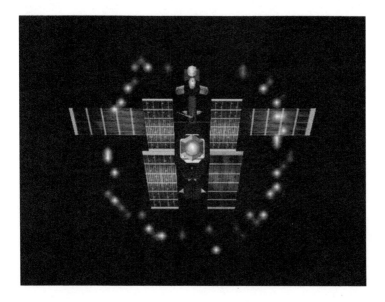

Hell, the damn camera could even betray you from time to time, but that comes with the territory when you're the first at something. It at least had a decent checkpoint system, though punishing always made me feel like it was my fault.

That's how games used to be; they would beat you down until you got good and rose to the occasion. It also had multiple endings to challenge you to go back and play it again, and frankly, it was just the only game like it for its time. That alone makes it a must buy for any Nintendo 64 owner.

OGRE BATTLE 64: PERSON OF LORDLY CALIBER (2000)

For me, tactical RPGs are some of the most exciting games from my childhood, and *Ogre Battle 64* was spawned from the legacy of the best. Specifically called *Ogre Battle 64: Person of Lordly Caliber*, it is a prime example of blending the epic story RPGs from the Super Nintendo generation with the 3-D graphics of the newest generation of gaming. When I consider the elaborate classes, items, and strategies at my disposal, there isn't a better RPG on the console. Black Knights, Dragoons, Angels... the available classes were elaborate and interesting.

When organizing the units across the 3x3 grid, I would essentially be preparing for every encounter imaginable. But unlike most RPGs in this time period, you don't actually participate in the battle. Everything is automated. So the focus is on finding appropriate matchups, understanding the enemy, and prepping for each encounter. I would even position my units on the world map in order to gain the advantage on other units by attacking from a direction they wouldn't expect.

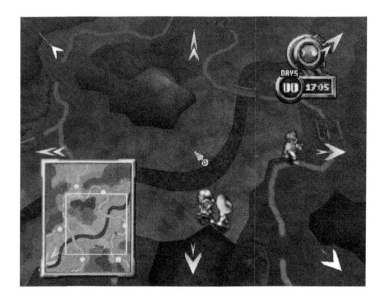

The epiphany I had when playing *Ogre Battle 64* back in the day came with the realization of just how different each playthrough could actually be. There were various "hero" characters who would join your party based on your accomplishments and the decisions you made along your journey.

Throw in the wild system where you could recruit all manner of bestiary and even enemy units. *Ogre Battle*

64 to this day has one of the deepest RPG systems and simplest combat mechanics in one package. My first playthrough was about 50 hours, but the second playthrough was easily more than a hundred hours. Now I know some of you are whining about the lack of any "real" combat, but you're missing the point. RPGs are about progress and statistics. It's about building this unstoppable force that you unleash onto an enemy and letting the machine do the work.

In *Ogre Battle 64*, I engineer the downfall of kingdoms and rise of my name through the land as my angels and ninjas raze the enemy strongholds. Tell me that doesn't sound like the perfect roleplaying experience.

SHAUN

Shaun Bolen is a show writer, personality, and community manager at ScrewAttack. He's played vidja games since the NES, but his addiction was solidified when he received a hand-me-down Sega Genesis from his older brother. The Nintendo 64 taught him valuable lessons in 3-D platforming, growing from boy to teenager, and entirely ignoring the left-side grip of the N64 controller.

@ShaunBolen

STAR WARS EPISODE I: RACER (1999)

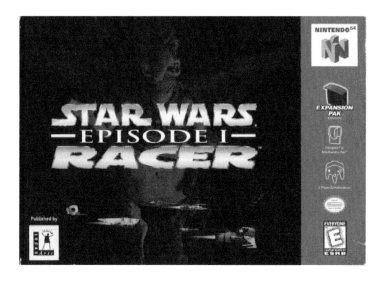

"They have podracing on Malastare. Very fast. Very dangerous." Qui-Gon was a wise man, and if LucasArts was going to make a video game out of arguably the only good part of the prequel trilogy, they knew the Master Jedi's words had to come across through the N64 controller. They accomplished just that with *Star Wars Episode I: Racer*. Whether swinging through the canyons of Tatooine or launching from the top of Howler Gorge, *Episode I: Racer* was fast and furious before Vin Diesel even thought about popping wheelies in a Dodge Charger.

I remember being SO scared playing this. Races were LONG — some hitting 10 minutes – with lengthy laps, dangerous turns, and an AI that loved to keep hot on your tail. However, the real magic that made it a classic were the underlying mechanics. Like Anakin from the film, your engines had to be watched carefully. Damage taken from collisions had to be repaired by holding the R button, which slowed down your speed drastically, forcing you to choose carefully when you needed to fix up your ride mid-race.

The boost, on the other hand, was more than simply holding a single button. When reaching your top speed, you had to press up on the stick, wait for it to charge, then press A again at the peak of your speedometer. It felt JUST like Anakin slamming his handlebars forward in his pod. You never feel in complete control in *Episode I: Racer*. It's a constant, ludicrous race of gambles, quick thinking, and maybe even luck. Coupled with awesome sound design from the film and a score that ramped up on the 3rd lap (like another certain racer featuring a mustached plumber in a go-cart), I now know EXACTLY how dangerous podracing is.

MARIO TENNIS
(2000)

There are definitely some other *Mario* spinoffs in this book, but I'd argue that *Mario Tennis* is the best one out there. *Mario Party* might have the politics and backstabbing that made it an immortal classic, but *Mario Tennis*' simplicity and emphasis on raw skill makes it the go-to for me. The original *Mario Tennis* didn't really have the emphasis on power-ups that the newer ones do — it was a purer game that made slamming in your friend's faces a raw showcase of how much they SUCK.

Doubles, which were supposed to be a team sport, quickly would turn into a free-for-all, as teammates would intentionally whiff to spite any failures that their partner committed. I didn't have an N64 originally, but I grew up with a set of identical twins named Collin and Taylor. They were cute, goofy, curly-headed boys, and while *Mario Party* was always a great time, sometimes we didn't have the time to invest in long plays, and *Mario Tennis* was so much better for quick sessions. I'd ALWAYS make sure the twins were on the same team during doubles because, quite frankly, there was nothing sillier than watching two look-alikes scream at each other when I'd kick the shit out of them in a tennis game as a ginormous gorilla. Plus it was the game where Waluigi made his debut, but most probably don't give a crap about him.

SUPER MARIO 64 (1996)

Super Mario 64 is a perfect game. I'm very sorry for putting it so frankly, but it's the only way I can articulate everything that this game gets right. For younger gamers reading this, I wish more than anything that there were a way for you to understand what it was like to play this game when it released in 1996.

It was the first of its kind — a truly open world 3-D platformer, and somehow Nintendo got more right than many developers could hope to today. It's like Nintendo invented the wheel, but rather than it being made of crude stone, they went ahead and constructed an entire Mercedes Benz. I'm not trying to sound like a 27-year-old claiming "all games were so much better back in the day," but no one has sunken a buzzer-beater or hit a walk-off grand slam the way that Nintendo nailed everything in this game. The soundtrack, visuals, physics, level design, difficulty, power-ups, and bosses are the stuff of legend.

It's not only perfect in the past tense. It's now perfect. As it exists today. From the very first screen, the one of Mario's face, the bar was set at perfection. The format, jumping through paintings as a level select, swimming with a giant eel in Jolly Roger Bay, spinning and throwing Bowser into bombs, foot-racing giant Koopas, exploring pyramids, finding ENTIRE WORLDS that could have been missed if you didn't explore. It's magic. It's an adventure. It's cryptic, and tough, and fair, and at its time, in an entirely new dimension.

In 1996 it was something unlike any gamer had experienced before. I can't stress enough what it did for the Nintendo 64 or any gamer that has or will play it in their lifetime.

STAR WARS: SHADOWS OF THE EMPIRE

(1996)

Let's discuss *Shadows of the Empire* and not talk about the snowspeeder sequence. It seems to be the only thing people remember this game for — and that's because they must have sucked at it and couldn't get past that first stage. But I found it particularly easy, even as an 8-year-old. *Shadows* has so much more to offer than a lackluster battle on Hoth—and that's a moment that no other *Star Wars* game in history has been able to recreate. This includes one-on-ones against AT-STs, surviving the hellish trains of Ord

Mantell, and, oh yeah, chasing down those dirtbags on speeder bikes through Beggar's Canyon.

I think most gamers of today would say that the quality of *Shadows of the Empire* is locked away in the nostalgia of those who played it. They'd call it a dated third-person shooter with horrible controls, and in all of their pretentiousness, would fail to name another game where they engaged in a one-on-one jetpack-and-laser duel with Boba Fett — something Han Solo sure as hell never did.

BEETLE ADVENTURE RACING (1999)

Mount Mayhem might be my favorite race track in any video game I've ever played. There's a section of a large suspension bridge under construction on the track and at this spot you can launch your car at some attack helicopters (that are there for I don't know what), and IF you don't collide with them, you'll fall a thousand feet, landing inside of a huge crystal cavern that is home to an enormous crashed UFO. Sounds great, right?!

When I was 11 back in 1999, I didn't care that this was a racing game that featured only VW Beetles – I cared about the quality of the game. I've been trying forever to understand what it was about *Beetle Adventure Racing* that made me love it SO much. The cars had real weight to them, the music was comprised of some pretty solid breakbeats, and it had plenty of personality, but it was the level design that made it so great. It took that mentality of kart racers — you know, themed tracks with outrageous jumps, shortcuts, and power-ups — and applied it to realistic locations.

I remember specifically there was an island-ish track that heavily resembled Jurassic Park, and at every lap through the Tyrannosaur paddock, something was getting closer. On the third lap, a HUGE T-Rex would burst out of the jungle over the path. To me as a kid, hell, to me as a 27-year-old, that's the really fun stuff. That's what gets inside your imagination as a gamer and stays there for decades.

EXTREME-G (1997)

I didn't realize half the games I volunteered to write about were racers, especially on the N64. Somehow racing games aren't typically the first thing I think about when gaming on the console — but I think that *Extreme-G* (and the other two I've ranted about already) are real testaments to what the transition to the third dimension did for the genre. I really didn't play racers until the N64 came out, and I really didn't love racers until I played *Extreme-G*.

I'd personally say its sequels were better games. In those you could go so fast that the sound barrier would break and all you would hear is a slight breeze of wind passing over as you raced at more than 750 MPH, but I don't remember those games like I remember the original *Extreme-G* because of how fresh it felt. It was bright and colorful, and I used to love the way that weapons would jettison in and hover close to your bike. When you'd get a pickup for a rocket launcher, for example, it would swoop in and hover above your cycle, almost attaching, and would detach after being used. It may not seem like much now, but that was so cool when I was a kid.

It had a trance soundtrack like the *Mortal Kombat* movie. It had motorcycles like *Tron*. It had courses like *F-Zero*. It had power-ups like *Mario Kart*, and it had a speed faster than anything I'd ever played before. I couldn't even keep up with what was happening on-screen. I can't tell you how I beat it. Its pace was so blistering I mostly just held on to my sweaty controller and prayed I came out on top. But more than anything, I just remember being a kid, playing four-player battle races with my best buddies and thinking damn . . . I should really slow down. That's a racing game.

THE VAULT

- [ ] Perfect Dark   ☆ ☆ ☆ ☆ ☆
- [ ] Pokémon Snap   ☆ ☆ ☆ ☆ ☆
- [ ] Legend Of Zelda: Ocarina Of Time   ☆ ☆ ☆ ☆ ☆
- [ ] Super Smash Bros   ☆ ☆ ☆ ☆ ☆
- [ ] Mario Party 2   ☆ ☆ ☆ ☆ ☆
- [ ] Pokémon Stadium   ☆ ☆ ☆ ☆ ☆
- [ ] Star Fox 64   ☆ ☆ ☆ ☆ ☆
- [ ] BattleTanx   ☆ ☆ ☆ ☆ ☆
- [ ] Bomberman 64   ☆ ☆ ☆ ☆ ☆
- [ ] Fighting Force 64   ☆ ☆ ☆ ☆ ☆
- [ ] WCW/nWo Revenge   ☆ ☆ ☆ ☆ ☆
- [ ] 1080° Snowboarding   ☆ ☆ ☆ ☆ ☆
- [ ] Buck Bumble   ☆ ☆ ☆ ☆ ☆
- [ ] Conker's Bad Fur Day   ☆ ☆ ☆ ☆ ☆
- [ ] Diddy Kong Racing   ☆ ☆ ☆ ☆ ☆
- [ ] GoldenEye 007   ☆ ☆ ☆ ☆ ☆
- [ ] Mario Party   ☆ ☆ ☆ ☆ ☆
- [ ] Rush 2: Extreme Racing USA   ☆ ☆ ☆ ☆ ☆
- [ ] Cruis'n USA   ☆ ☆ ☆ ☆ ☆
- [ ] Mario Kart 64   ☆ ☆ ☆ ☆ ☆
- [ ] NBA Hangtime   ☆ ☆ ☆ ☆ ☆
- [ ] NFL Blitz 2000   ☆ ☆ ☆ ☆ ☆
- [ ] Yoshi's Story   ☆ ☆ ☆ ☆ ☆

- ☐ Banjo-Kazooie — ☆ ☆ ☆ ☆ ☆
- ☐ Legend Of Zelda: Majora's Mask — ☆ ☆ ☆ ☆ ☆
- ☐ Kirby 64: The Crystal Shards — ☆ ☆ ☆ ☆ ☆
- ☐ Blast Corps — ☆ ☆ ☆ ☆ ☆
- ☐ Donkey Kong 64 — ☆ ☆ ☆ ☆ ☆
- ☐ F-Zero X — ☆ ☆ ☆ ☆ ☆
- ☐ Harvest Moon 64 — ☆ ☆ ☆ ☆ ☆
- ☐ Jet Force Gemini — ☆ ☆ ☆ ☆ ☆
- ☐ Pilotwings 64 — ☆ ☆ ☆ ☆ ☆
- ☐ Snowboard Kids — ☆ ☆ ☆ ☆ ☆
- ☐ Star Wars: Rogue Squadron — ☆ ☆ ☆ ☆ ☆
- ☐ Gauntlet Legends — ☆ ☆ ☆ ☆ ☆
- ☐ Hydro Thunder — ☆ ☆ ☆ ☆ ☆
- ☐ Turok: Dinosaur Hunter — ☆ ☆ ☆ ☆ ☆
- ☐ Wave Race 64 — ☆ ☆ ☆ ☆ ☆
- ☐ WinBack: Covert Operations — ☆ ☆ ☆ ☆ ☆
- ☐ Ogre Battle 64: Person of Lordly Caliber — ☆ ☆ ☆ ☆ ☆
- ☐ Star Wars Episode I: Racer — ☆ ☆ ☆ ☆ ☆
- ☐ Mario Tennis — ☆ ☆ ☆ ☆ ☆
- ☐ Super Mario 64 — ☆ ☆ ☆ ☆ ☆
- ☐ Star Wars: Shadows Of The Empire — ☆ ☆ ☆ ☆ ☆
- ☐ Beetle Adventure Racing — ☆ ☆ ☆ ☆ ☆
- ☐ Extreme-G — ☆ ☆ ☆ ☆ ☆

AUTHOR BIO

Hi, we're the ScrewAttack crew. We've been making original videos online since February 2006! You know what internet video looked like in 2006? Cat videos and guys getting hit in the nuts. Yeah, things sure have changed. We have a lot of great people who work at ScrewAttack but the fine gents who helped write this book are Craig Skistimas, Bryan Baker, Nick Cramer, Chad James, Shaun Bolen, Sam Mitchell, Ben Singer, Sean Hinz, and Austin Harper.

In addition to making tons of videos for our website and YouTube channel, we also throw a massive party every year called "SGC." It's been labeled "The Biggest Party in Gaming" so if you ever get a chance to come hang out with us we'd love to meet you.

Someday we hope that someone who's really rich will see our "talents" and deliver us a giant bag of money with a dollar sign on it. Until that day we'll keep playing video games and making fun videos for you... And now writing books!

CPSIA information can be obtained
at www.ICGtesting.com
Printed in the USA
BVOW10s2253050616

450629BV00001B/1/P